The Renters Blueprint

TURNING RENTERS INTO HOMEOWNERS

Erica Smith

Note from the Author

So many renters want to invest in Real Estate but they're not sure how the process works. As a Real Estate Professional, it is my responsibility to help educate you on the home buying experience, so you can have a successful closing on your first property. This book will walk you through the steps that you can expect on this journey. Let me show you how to gain generational wealth for your family's future.

Table of Content

- Introduction
- Step 1: Create a Real Estate Plan
- Step 2: Review Your Finances
- Step 3: Let's Talk Credit
- Step 4: Financing
- Step 5: Getting Approved
- Step 6: Hiring a Realtor
- Step 7: House Shopping
- Step 8: You've found Your New Home! Now What?
- Step 9: It's Closing Time
- Step 10: Congratulations! You're a Home Owner
- Resources

"The best way to predict the future is to create it."

~Peter Drucker

Step One

Create a Real Estate Plan

Buying a house is a big decision and a serious commitment. You'll need to get in the mindset of a Homeowner and not a Renter. Determine your short and long term goals as it relates to purchasing a home and create a realistic plan based on your goals.

Ask Yourself:
- Do you want to buy an investment property or primary residence?
- If you purchase a rental property, do you want to live in one apartment and rent the other(s)?
- Where is the desired location you want to live in?
- How much do you want or need to save for your down payment?
- Are you paying cash or financing?
- Have you considered your loan options and down payment requirements?

These are some of the things you need to consider when creating your plan. You have to set an obtainable goal or it will be just that, A GOAL! Trust the process. Try not to get discouraged and I promise the reward will be great.

Notes

Notes

"If you're not going to put money in real estate, where else?"

~Tamir Sapir

Step Two

Review Your Finances

Once you've established a plan and set your goals, review your financial situation. What is your budget? Know how much you can afford for your monthly mortgage. You should also take into consideration all recurring monthly expenses.

Know your out of pocket upfront expenses...
- Do you have earnest money? Earnest Money is a part of your down payment that you pay upon offer acceptance.
- Do you have money for a home inspection? This is paid at the time of inspection usually the first 5-7 days of offer acceptance.
- Do you have money for an appraisal? This is scheduled and ordered by the mortgage company.

Do you have money for your down payment? It can be 0%-20% depending on your loan type. You should also have at minimum two months of reserves saved up.

Notes

Notes

Step Three

Let's Talk Credit

Credit is the most important step to home ownership. Your credit score determines your interest rate, loan type and any available down payment assistance programs that may be available for you. Mortgage lenders look at your credit score and payment history. Lenders want to know if you have a history of paying your bills on time. The best way to build your credit score quickly is to get a secured credit card from your bank and use it responsibly. They will report payments to all major credit bureaus on a monthly basis. As long as you maintain payments on time and keep the balance low, your credit score will improve.

You should check your credit report regularly. Sign up for a free credit monitoring service, they will notify you about any changes to your credit. You want to verify that all accounts are being reported correctly. If you find any inaccurate information, contact the credit bureaus or the actual creditor immediately.

Let's Talk Credit

Here are some tips to help improve your credit:

- Pay your bills on time: Any late or missed payments can lower your credit score. Paying on time consistently can boost your score
- Pay off debt and keep balances low on all credit cards
- Dispute all inaccuracies on your credit report immediately
- Do not close unused credit cards, keep them open and at a minimum balance
- Do not obtain new credit inquiries

Delinquencies can remain on your credit report for up to 7 years.

Notes

Notes

"Don't think about it's current value. Think about it's future value."

~Anonymous

Step Four

Financing

There are different types of mortgage loans. The most commonly used are FHA, VA and Conventional loans. When shopping for a mortgage ask questions. This will help you understand the process so you'll get the best terms for your home loan. The lender will review your finances and credit worthiness to determine how much home you can afford.

Let's look at the different loan types and requirements..
Federal Housing Administration (FHA) is the easiest home loan to get because it is designed for low to moderate income borrowers, requires a lower minimum down payment and lower credit score.
FHA loans
- Property must be your primary residence
- Requires 3.5% down payment of purchase price
- Mortgage Insurance Premiums are required
- Borrower must have proof of employment

Financing

Veteran Affairs (VA) is a loan that benefits veteran military service members and some surviving spouses. You can apply for a VA loan through a bank or mortgage company. The process is similar to applying for other mortgages. The only difference is you will need a certificate of eligibility (COE) to show that you meet the requirements for the VA loan.

VA loan
- No minimum credit score to qualify
- No down payment; 100% financing
- Borrower pays closing costs
- No private mortgage insurance
- Proof of employment

Financing

Conventional Loans have stricter requirements but are a good option if you have solid credit. Conventional mortgages can require a larger down payment than other types of loans. They traditionally require up to 20% down payment.

Conventional loan:
- Requires a higher credit score to qualify
- Requires mortgage insurance unless you are putting 20% down of the purchase price
- In some cases, minimum down payment is 3%
- Can be used to purchase a primary residence or an investment property

Notes

Notes

"Don't let the fear of losing be greater than the excitement of winning."

~Robert Kiyosaki

Step Five

Getting Approved

Applying for a mortgage can be exciting and also confusing. Getting pre-qualified or pre-approved for a mortgage is necessary. For starters, you'll need to fill out a mortgage application. Lenders look at key factors like your credit worthiness, employment history and income. Assets, liabilities and your debt-to-income ratio are also considered. Pre-qualifications and pre-approvals are not the same. A pre-qualification can be used to estimate how much you can afford to spend on a home. With some basic financial information, lenders can pre-qualify you right away. On the other hand, a pre-approval requires you to give the lender more detailed financial information like tax returns, check stubs and bank statements. Most sellers expect buyers to already have a pre-approval letter from their lender and will be more willing to negotiate if you do.

Notes

Notes

"If you think hiring a pro is expensive wait till you hire an amateur."

~Red Adair

Step Six

Hiring a Realtor

When hiring a Realtor, you should interview about 2-3 realtors. There are many steps to the home buying process and it can get complicated. Make sure you select the Realtor that's best for you. A reliable realtor can make home shopping easier and less stressful. A realtor should represent your interests. Your realtor will negotiate the price, sale conditions and help you avoid paying too much for the property. Once you've hired your realtor, they will discuss your must haves and wants, search for properties and send them to you for your review. Realtors will also schedule showings for properties that you are interested in. You may see many houses before you find your dream home, but when you find "the one" you'll be ready to make an offer!

Notes

Notes

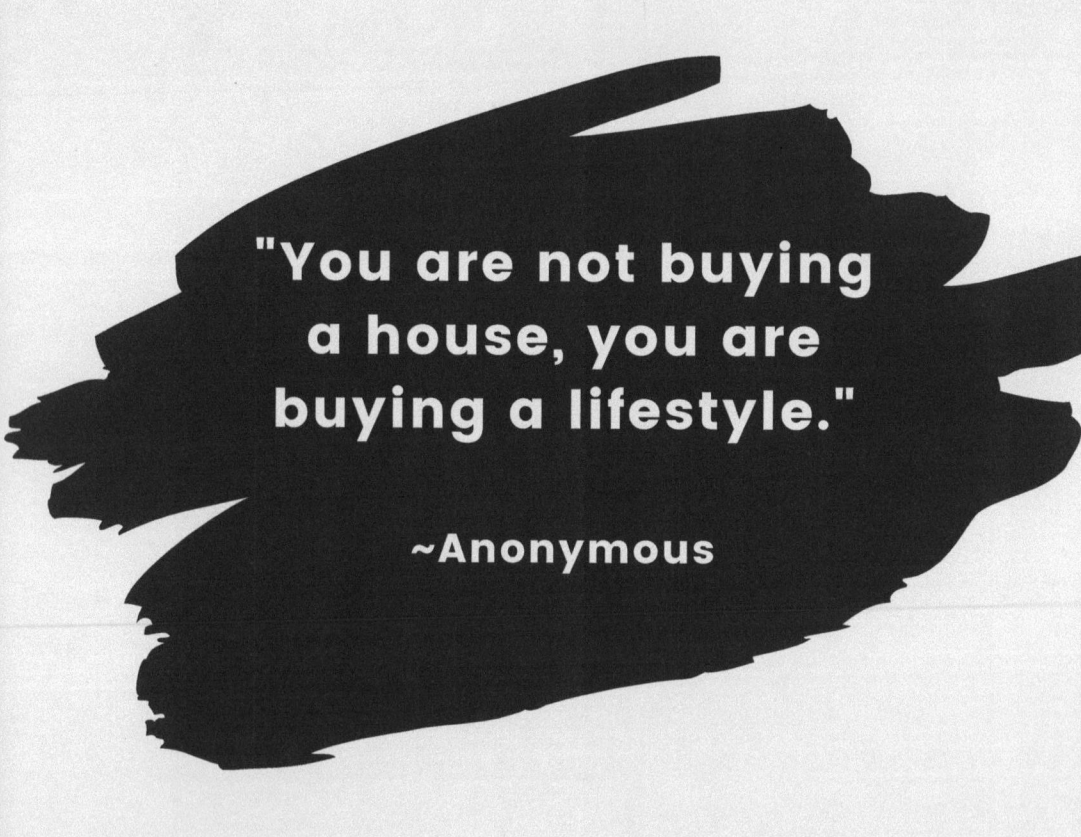

Step Seven

House Shopping

House Hunting is the most exciting part of the homebuying process. Take as much time as you need to find the right one. You'll see many houses, so I suggest you make a wish list of must haves and things you would like to have.

- Must have - you absolutely need it
- Want to have - are wishes but aren't at the top of your list
- Deal Breakers - if a home doesn't have it you immediately take it off the list

Browse available homes online to get a feel for your local housing market and how much the average home sells for in your area. Start by touring open houses and homes in your price range. Compare prices of what's on the market to your budget. Location is important when deciding which home to buy. Drive around the neighborhood that you think you may like or want to live in. Find the home that makes you happy and will accommodate your family, but be sure to stick to your budget. Finding the right home can take some time, if you can picture yourself in the home or start to think about where to put furniture or what color schemes you want, that's a good sign that this may be the one. When you find the one that fits your needs, be prepared to make a strong offer.

Notes

Notes

"There's no place like home."

~L. Frank Baum

Step Eight

YOU'VE FOUND YOUR HOME
NOW WHAT?

When you find your home and your offer is accepted, there are a few things you should do right away...

- Get your earnest money ready
- Get a Home Inspection: Even if the property is sold AS-IS. The inspector introduces you to the property and determines if any repairs are needed. They will go through the property from top to bottom, letting you know what's right and wrong with the property.
- Hire a real estate attorney: Real estate deals can be tricky, so it's best to have an attorney to protect your interests. The real estate attorney will review the contract and advocate on your behalf. Some states require a real estate attorney and others do not. Hiring an attorney is recommended for legal advice.

If you are financing your home, the lender might request more documents from you during this time. The lender will also order an appraisal for the property. The appraisal is used to determine what your property is worth. The appraiser will inspect the property then compare it with sold comparable houses in the neighborhood to assess the fair market value of the property.

Notes

Notes

"Live for the moment you can't put in words."

~Anonymous

Step Nine

IT'S CLOSING TIME

You've found your forever home and the bank has approved your loan. Now, it's closing time!

The Closing will involve lots of paperwork and signatures. Bring your photo ID and certified funds to cover your down payment and closing cost and be sure to be on time. Before the actual closing of the deal, you should complete a final walk through of the property to make sure the property is in the same condition or better than your initial visit. This typically happens 24 hours before the closing.

During the closing you will receive the deed to the property naming you as the new owner. You will receive a statement listing all costs related to the property sale for the buyer and seller. If you have an attorney, they will review the paperwork with you. Ask questions if there's something you don't understand.

Once all the paperwork is signed, mortgage has funded with the title company, and closing is official, you will receive the keys to the property.

Notes

Notes

"A house is made of brick and mortar, but home is made by the people who live there."

~M.K.Soni

Step Ten

CONGRATULATIONS!!
YOU'RE A HOMEOWNER

The first thing you should do is store all your documents from the closing in a safe place. If you haven't already done so, you can now change your address, contact your utility services, and change the locks. Start looking ahead and planning for expenses that will go toward any upgrades for your new property like painting, replacing window treatments, light fixtures and appliances.

Notes

Notes

Resources

HOMEBUYER RESOURCES

- www.Linktr.ee/EricaSellsHouses

- www..AnnualCreditReport.com

- www.CreditKarma.com

- www.HUD.gov

- www.LegalShield.com

About the Author

Erica Smith Morrow

A License Managing Broker, Notary Public, PSA, e-Pro, started her real estate career in 2000 as Property Manager and an apartment finder. She has a wealth of knowledge and expertise about how the rental and the home buying process unfolds. When the market changed, owning became easier and more profitable than renting. Thus, Erica began her journey of turning renters into homeowners.

Erica establishes a strong and lasting relationship with her clients. Whether you are a renter, first-time home buyer or seller she will walk you through the steps of the process. If you are selling, Erica will get the property sold faster since she has a pool of preapproved buyers that are educated on what it takes to become a homeowner. She's there to assist her clients from the beginning of the process, to the deal closing. Her goal is to turn your real estate dream into reality as stress free as possible.

linktr.ee/ericasellshouses

www.ingramcontent.com/pod-product-compliance
Lightning Source LLC
Chambersburg PA
CBHW040245220526
45473CB00001B/374